Trust~in~God
Therapy

Trust~in~God Therapy

written by
Carol Ann Morrow

illustrated by
R.W. Alley

A ONE
CARING
PLACE
Abbey Press

Text © 1998 by Carol Ann Morrow
Illustrations © 1998 by St. Meinrad Archabbey
Published by One Caring Place
Abbey Press
St. Meinrad, Indiana 47577

Library of Congress Catalog Number
98-73408

ISBN 978-0-87029-322-1

Printed in the United States of America

Foreword

I have long been urged by friends and spiritual guides to trust in God, and I have long tried to do so. At times, I have succeeded. But at other times, I have withheld that trust—or offered it and taken it back, stumbling around on my own. And I've often wondered: Is trust something I give to God or something God gives to me?

I've decided it's both. Trust in God is both gift *and* choice, grace *and* effort. It may not help anyone find a parking space or pay the utility bill—it's not a religious rabbit's foot. But it can bring us the clarity to understand, the courage to seize the opportunity, the serenity to wait when waiting is all we can do.

I've also come to realize that the more we practice the "therapy" of trust in God, the stronger our spiritual muscles will grow. So I invite you to join with me in holding each little thought in this book as a spiritual exercise. Stretch it, struggle with it, cry it, pray it.

Trust in God is possible. Trust in God is wisdom. Trust in God.

1.

No matter what you have
known of doubt, fear, or
betrayal, you are here today—
right where you need to be.
Trust the strong thread that ties
your life's moments together.
It is spun of Love.

2.

Choose to be like a wild daisy or a field sparrow. Greet the dawn, confident that you have all you need to be what you are meant to be. When the day brings storm or drought, bird and flower hold on bravely to life. Simply trust. Trust simply.

3.

God wants only the best for you. The path may not be easy, smooth, short, or detour-free. But it will get you where you need to be—with God as your constant companion.

4.

Trust tunes you to the
wavelength of the music of
the universe. Listen...and the
harmonies of life will become
more apparent to you.

5.

Trust stands tall, eyes awake to
see, arms extended, hands open
to receive the good. Assume the
posture of trust.

6.

Be welcoming, not wary.
Expect gifts, not troubles.
Anticipate the many disguises
of grace and prepare to recognize
them as they appear.

7.

You may learn dependence on God by first trusting a friend or a spouse, or sharing the journey of someone else who struggles. Have faith that God will send you the guides you need.

8.

Practice awareness of God in times of blessing, so that God's presence is familiar in times of trouble. Recognize and reverence God's many manifestations: in nature, in other people, in unexpected places, in unlikely miracles.

9.

Practice words of trust: "I believe." "I am confident." "I am not afraid." These bold sentences will build bridges across the crevasses of fear in your mind, heart, and soul.

10.

You may learn to rely on God from practicing faith. Or you may grasp the truth of trust as you hang by the fingernails of one hand from a spiritual precipice. Some people, at some times, seem to require more homework. Hang on!

11.

Within your body and soul,
God has planted seeds of trust.
Most people can trust their
heart to beat and their lungs
to fill. More importantly,
everyone can come to know
what is good and holy. Let
the holiness within you guide
your quest for trust in God.

12.

Practice the prayer of trust.
Lie back on the ground or rest
in a chair with your hands
held open on your lap. Let your
whole body say, "I will allow
God's truth to emerge in my
life. I am ready."

13.

Faith expects life to reveal its goodness. Fear dreads the approach of the day. You can feel the effects of fear in your body. Let yourself fall into God's embrace.

14.

You trust the sun and the moon and the tides. You believe that God has a plan for melting day into night, for turning the seasons of the year. Would God fail to have a plan for you?

15.

You trust in electricity, plumbing, alarm clocks. You trust traffic lights, bus and plane schedules, the refrigerator and the furnace. All these fail. God is more worthy of your trust than the weather forecaster! Back into trust, if you must.

16.

If you can't begin by believing in God's love for you, begin by believing that the earth's surface can support your weight while gravity keeps you from floating off. In the simplest actions, you reveal considerable trust.

17.

Trust does not make us immune to trouble. Bad things do happen to trusting people. But it can give us something to hold on to when life is crumbling around us. Hold on, hold fast, hold out!

18.

It's true God works in mysterious ways—but often through natural processes, ordinary people, normal events. Look for things falling into place, truth dawning, healing happening. Believe in everyday miracles!

19.

In whom have you placed your trust? Picture God as that person—your grandma, your coach, your kindergarten teacher. Trust God in the ways you trusted that person—to bandage your wounds, dry your tears, lead you on new paths.

20.

Confide one of your doubts or
fears to a loved one. Or ask a
favor of someone you know.
When human beings respond
with generosity and goodwill,
you get the smallest hint of the
good God wants for you.

21.

When you visit the valley
of the shadows, do not go
empty-handed. To face a single
terror, you need at least ten
memories of trust honored,
of good experienced. Rehearse
and store those memories now
against the dark times of the
future.

22.

Trust can be broken—or bent to the breaking point—by the actions of others. You can despair or you can reaffirm your faith in the basic goodness of people and the power of God to heal all wounds.

23.

Trust is tested by doubt—
which can be triggered by pain
or betrayal, hardship or loss.
In times of doubt, remember
past faithfulness and blessings
and anticipate new ones. Know
that God can transform trial
into triumph.

24.

When roads come to an end, planes crash, babies die, crops fail, or houses burn, God is present. Yet God is not the dead end, the crash, the death, the failure, or the fire. Look to God to find power in the midst of pain, to turn loss to gain, to make ends into beginnings.

25.

We can have confidence that creation is unfolding according to God's will, but we can also help to make it so. Use your special gifts to bring kindness, peace, and healing to a world in need.

26.

Faith means searching for the
divine plan in events that bless
us as well as events that try our
souls. This is the seesaw truth
of trust—to sense God's hand
in both turmoil and tranquility.
Hold on tight through the ups
and downs of life.

27.

Help God help you. As a
proverb says, "Call on God,
but row away from the rocks."
Do what you need to do.
Paddle in the right direction.

28.

Resignation and trust are not twins. Resignation bows under the weight. Trust simply waits. Trust as a child does—with innocence and confidence and anticipation of the good that is to come.

29.

If you decide to rely completely on your own power to work out life's dilemmas, God will not somehow revoke your heavenly insurance policy. You are always loved dearly. Count on God to be infinitely patient.

30.

Trust is not just an attitude. Trust acts. Wait in trust, and you wait with hope. Act in trust, and you open yourself to divine action and abundance in your life.

31.

A world without trust is unreliable, unruly, and inhospitable. A life without trust is tiny, timid, and tense. Place your hand in God's, to ensure against a life and a world too narrow for love.

32.

Depending on God isn't foolishness or fancy. It isn't laissez-faire or lackadaisical. It both requires and creates courage. Be strong!

33.

Faith relieves us of the burdens imposed both by the past and the future. Trust...and you will find yourself in the present— and the Presence of God.

34.

Faith requires that we rely on the invisible. What can be seen may appear to fall short of a blessing. Yet grace is as strong as gravity. Rely on the Almighty, and you will find yourself pulled toward heaven as certainly as gravity pulls you toward earth.

35.

Just because you don't feel serene and enlightened all the time doesn't mean you've flunked Trust-in-God 101. Sometimes feelings lag behind. Go through the motions—walk the walk, talk the talk, pray the prayer until the sense of God-with-you returns. Trust in trust.

36.

Trust is not spiritual equipment to be used only in case of crisis—like a parachute or an airbag. Reliance on God is an expression of truth, a set of your soul, a way of life. Trust God whenever...whatever... wherever...forever.

37.

God trusts you. God delights in
your desire to strengthen your
faith. Every movement of your
searching heart is a holy gift.
Believe in the quest itself.

38.

God invites, "Trust me!" What will you reply? Could you really say, "Not today," or "Let me give it some more thought," or "Why should I?" Or will you simply whisper, "Teach me to trust; I am afraid, but I place my hand in yours"?

Carol Ann Morrow is the author of *Peace Therapy,* also published by Abbey Press, and the founding editor of *Youth Update,* a publication for teens from St. Anthony Messenger Press. While she was writing this book, her mother became ill. This led her to reflect on the great trust required of her mother, who married and moved far from home to mother nine children, including baby Lara, who died on Mother's Day. Carol Ann honors that trust.

Illustrator for the Abbey Press Elf-help Books, **R.W. Alley** also illustrates and writes children's books. He lives in Barrington, Rhode Island, with his wife, daughter, and son. See a wide variety of his works at: www.rwalley.com.

The Story of the Abbey Press Elves

The engaging figures that populate the Abbey Press "elf-help" line of publications and products first appeared in 1987 on the pages of a small self-help book called *Be-good-to-yourself Therapy*. Shaped by the publishing staff's vision and defined in R.W. Alley's inventive illustrations, they lived out author Cherry Hartman's gentle, self-nurturing advice with charm, poignancy, and humor.

Reader response was so enthusiastic that more Elf-help Books were soon under way, a still-growing series that has inspired a line of related gift products.

The especially endearing character featured in the early books—sporting a cap with a mood-changing candle in its peak—has since been joined by a spirited female elf with flowers in her hair.

These two exuberant, sensitive, resourceful, kindhearted, lovable sprites, along with their lively elfin community, reveal what's truly important as they offer messages of joy and wonder, playfulness and co-creation, wholeness and serenity, the miracle of life and the mystery of God's love.

With wisdom and whimsy, these little creatures with long noses demonstrate the elf-help way to a rich and fulfilling life.

Elf-help Books

...adding "a little character" and a lot
of help to self-help reading!

Book price is \$4.95 unless otherwise noted.
Available at your favorite gift shop or bookstore—
or directly from One Caring Place, Abbey Press
Publications, St. Meinrad, IN 47577.
Or call 1-800-325-2511.
www.carenotes.com